SPORTS JOURNAL #7: HOCKEY

Cool Image Press
2014

Sports Journal #7: Hockey

Blank Pages

Published by Cool Image Press, 2014

ISBN-13: 978-1494952150
ISBN-10: 1494952157

Sports Journal

Sports Journal

Sports Journal

Sports Journal

Sports Journal

Sports Journal

Sports Journal

Sports Journal

Sports Journal

Sports Journal

Sports Journal

Sports Journal

Sports Journal

Sports Journal

Sports Journal

Sports Journal

Sports Journal

Sports Journal

Sports Journal

Sports Journal

Sports Journal

Sports Journal

Sports Journal

Sports Journal

Sports Journal

Sports Journal

Sports Journal

Sports Journal

Sports Journal

Sports Journal

Sports Journal

Sports Journal

Sports Journal

Sports Journal

Sports Journal

Sports Journal

Sports Journal

Sports Journal

Sports Journal

Sports Journal

Sports Journal

Sports Journal

Sports Journal

Sports Journal

Sports Journal

Sports Journal

Sports Journal

Sports Journal

Sports Journal

Sports Journal

Sports Journal

Sports Journal

Sports Journal

Sports Journal

Sports Journal

Sports Journal

Sports Journal

Sports Journal

Sports Journal

Sports Journal

Sports Journal

Sports Journal

Sports Journal

Sports Journal

Sports Journal

Sports Journal

Sports Journal

Sports Journal

Sports Journal

Sports Journal

Sports Journal

Sports Journal

Sports Journal

Sports Journal

Sports Journal

Sports Journal

Sports Journal

Sports Journal

Sports Journal

Sports Journal

Sports Journal

Sports Journal

Sports Journal

Sports Journal

Sports Journal

Sports Journal

Sports Journal

Sports Journal

Sports Journal

Sports Journal

Sports Journal

Sports Journal

Sports Journal

Sports Journal

Sports Journal

Sports Journal

Sports Journal

Sports Journal

Sports Journal

Sports Journal

Sports Journal

Sports Journal

Sports Journal

Sports Journal

Sports Journal

Sports Journal

Sports Journal

Sports Journal

Sports Journal

Sports Journal

Sports Journal

Sports Journal

Sports Journal

Sports Journal

Sports Journal

Sports Journal

Sports Journal

Sports Journal

Sports Journal

Sports Journal

Sports Journal

Sports Journal

Sports Journal

Sports Journal

Sports Journal

Sports Journal

Sports Journal

Sports Journal

Sports Journal

Sports Journal

Sports Journal

Sports Journal

Sports Journal

Sports Journal

Sports Journal

Sports Journal

Sports Journal

Sports Journal

Sports Journal

Sports Journal

Sports Journal

Sports Journal

Sports Journal

Sports Journal

Sports Journal

Sports Journal

Sports Journal

Sports Journal

Sports Journal

Sports Journal

Sports Journal

Sports Journal

Sports Journal

Sports Journal

Sports Journal

Sports Journal

Sports Journal

Sports Journal

Sports Journal

Sports Journal

Sports Journal

Sports Journal

Sports Journal

Sports Journal

Sports Journal

Sports Journal

Sports Journal

Sports Journal

Sports Journal

Sports Journal

Sports Journal

Sports Journal

Sports Journal

Sports Journal

Sports Journal

Sports Journal

Sports Journal

Sports Journal

Sports Journal

Sports Journal

Sports Journal

Sports Journal

Sports Journal

Sports Journal

Sports Journal

Sports Journal

Sports Journal

Sports Journal

Sports Journal

Sports Journal

Sports Journal

Sports Journal

Sports Journal

Sports Journal

Sports Journal

Sports Journal

Sports Journal

Sports Journal

Sports Journal

Sports Journal

Made in the USA
Middletown, DE
28 May 2016